The
Last Exit

Terrence Davis

Author Photo by Ty Xavier Weldon

Dedicated with love to

My nephew Justin. I thank you for opening my eyes to see the truth. At the age of four, you made me see everything so clearly and I love you with all my heart.

Contents

Three
The Smoke Screen

Six
Closing Arguments

Foreword

Have you ever wanted to read poetry that touched you right where you were in life? Terrence Davis has created a collection of works that do more than just make mere words sound beautiful. His work encapsulates the voice of a person needing to vent. He has transposed every facet of himself onto pages that were once void of expression. From the moment I read the first piece I knew that he was not scared to be transparent. In reading his works I was reminded of my own realities and found comfort in knowing that another person knew exactly what I was feeling. Being a person that understands the joys of love and one who has survived the pains of that same word, I found this collection to be just what I needed to gain a fresh perspective on some of the things I have personally endured.

If you are one who loves to read about the complexities of life, then you will thoroughly enjoy the ride Terrence has created. A great number of his poems are wonderfully interwoven words that express how love can be the best feeling one moment and seconds later have you on the floor crying in the fetal position. Terrence has perfected the art of making readers look within themselves. His sharp and direct style will be appreciated by those ready to be enlightened. Each poem has prolific messages that are empowering to say the least. And even though this was not created to be a "self-help" book, it truly has the language to free the minds of those trapped by scars from their past.

The ever present trauma of urban living which seems to constantly miss the vicissitudes of life is painted perfectly in his poem *Spray Cans*, and an honest look at sexuality is bluntly depicted in *Animal Testing*. As refreshing as it was to read, I was also proud to see someone I call a friend being able to express himself in a manner that I know will be appreciated by the masses. There is definitely a need for more authors like Terrence and I am certain that this is only the beginning. After I read his poem entitled *Intervention*, there was nothing for me to say but wow because at one point in my life I was living with that same state of mind. Any reader of poetry old or new will respect his ability to target so many aspects of condition and bring to light those circumstances we hesitate to talk about. The way he tackles the hypersensitive topic of religion in *The Long Way Home* and *Til' Kingdom Comes* are certain to raise eyebrows and ruffle feathers even though the truth therein cannot be denied. Terrence has left no one untouched and unapologetically puts on paper the thoughts of many.

As a fellow author I commend Terrence on capturing my attention and keeping me excited through his words. I know how difficult it can be to vent on paper, leaving yourself open for all to view. However, I also know the importance of staying true to self and pushing the envelope so that change may occur. The Last Exit is a much needed wake-up call for those that need to be reminded that it is ok to feel, to love, to hurt and most importantly...to heal.

Dontá Morrison
Author, The *End of the Rainbow*

One

*Love Or
Something
Like It*

Resting Heart Rate

My doctor says I will never get over you
I still name my past, present and future after you
My hopes and dreams planned out for you
A line in the sand in a desert
With a coffin lying next to you
And truth is I'm never myself around you
You love this up and down in me
Controlling me like hoodoo
And I feel like we're in hell here
Trapped in a shell broken and abused
Both of us want to leave, need to leave
But being with you in our hell
Is a comfort zone for me
And there's no guessing baby
We are in a state of complacency
Living in a space where there
Should be a vacancy
So you should honor and trust
This place we are in
Trouble doesn't last always
You should feel comfort in the fact that
Getting rid of you right now is a distant memory
I get so high off of you pain and pleasure
Has become next of kin to me
Breaking me down because you were
Never a friend to me
And my heart should have warned me that
You're not half of what you pretend to be
I sought refuge in a place and

Lied in bed with the enemy
And yea, there's cause to argue
Where is my accountability?
Can't sweep in front of my own house
When you pull the rug from under me
Your comfort lies in just being under me
Can't understand why it took so long to realize
This rollercoaster is just not fun for me
Babysitting like you're a son to me
Can't deny you've always been a son of a b
Raised being all that you can be
Should've left when I found
I wasn't even on your list of priorities
A shift in responsibilities
No fun being last on the list
Right below the groceries
You've never really been close to me
I've been your brother, cousin, friend
None of what I'm supposed to be
Hung me like hangman from a tree
So what's the use in waving the white flag
When all you have to do is sit back and
Pretend to be in love with me?
No sense in letting this caged bird fly free
No use in bandaging these wounds
Especially when all you want to do is
Smile at the thought of watching me bleed
Lying to myself believing one day
This heart of mine will fulfill all your needs

Damage Control

What some call love we call infinity
Wanna layup with you cocoon style
Smelling the sweet spot
In between your neck
We relax and sit cross-legged
Camp fire style staring at
One another wondering
What will happen when the night ends
We are the pulse of two lovers
Who wait at home for us
Wondering when the love stopped
And where things went wrong
We share silent secrets
Thoughts to never be spoken
We are what love has become
Two people belonging to
Someone else who never
Had the courage to say it's over
So it's over

Haiku

They tell me of this
Thing called love, I'd rather have
Something tangible

Til' KINGDOM Comes

You one day Christians
Breathe, love and live in fiction
Eat, sleep, shit and breed lies with conviction
Couldn't fathom the truth would
Cause some friction
Recited sappy love poems with diction
Reeling me into your web of affliction
Tried to make me strung out on loves addiction
Every word came out of contradiction but
I was at least smart enough
To have some suspicions
Gave lock and key to your space
With no restrictions
But told me loving you had some conditions
Can't pump fast enough
Side effects from prescriptions
Everything with you fails just my prediction
Kingdom in G minor
Suitable enough for description
Didn't quite know how to make the transition
Could see the discomfort in your disposition
Had a gut wrenching gut feeling intuition
I was only being used for some silly ass competition
He loves me, he loves me not
Fallen petals off of a dead rose's superstition
Tried to make a space in your place
But the walls started closing in
And I could smell the scents of

Old lovers and lost men
Read the writings on the wall
Can't deny you wanted to be Barbie and Ken
A sneaky goose mother hen
Finally aired out the dirt with
A neighborhood friend
Everyone knows all about where you've been
A rogue dressing like a high priestess
Tried to get under my skin
Heard all about the lies you spread through the gen
Two side to a book
Two versions to defend
Truth lives where lies hide like a Siamese twin
Cried wolf on the phone queuing up the violin
Don't know which side is up
Don't know where to begin
And the only ones in your corner
The picture perfect imperfect pretend to be friends
Recognize this is one battle you will never win
Detonate the clef notes on your arm
And take it on the chin
You don't really want those
Church boys to know all about your sins
You freaks like to sneak with hide and seek paces
You left traces, nooks and crannies
To all your hidden places
Singing tunes, silent prayers and saving graces
And even that shit won't cover all the bases
Don't want the comeback choir knowing
You love the warmth of male embraces
Let's face it

You've been with many different names
A slew of different faces
You like the victim role, you like the chases
No one really thought you were ready for the races
The bitch in you only hunts for the tasting
A real hunter should know when to tuck his head
But you're so brazen
You deserve this ass whooping
So man up and take it
One life to live and you ought to save it
All that talent just to be wasted
This is what happens when you
Make a promise just to break it
It's a shame how complex bullshit
Becomes so basic
KINGDOM come, KINGDOM gone
Realizing that character out a book had two faces

I Love You Too

These words taste like
Poison and smell like fear
Allergic reaction to this
Binding glue so I'm
Throwing them back to you

Miss Me in Him

I met him zigzagging and free throwing
Swimming in a lake a mile long
With three bags of luggage
He's one year older than I was
When I was just a thought
And ten times as deep as I was
When I was just beat boxing
On dirty cafeteria tables
He's tailored, suited
And fitted to my needs
I'm knee deep in him
And I miss me in him
He's my king conqueror
The perfect verse after a hook

Finding Love

I've got these feelings for a girl
No strings attached
She coddles me like a live wire
While I sit in her lap
She's half white, half black
Maybe Korean depends where she's at
Its poetry unexplained
And I love her for that

Whisper

Don't think I didn't hear you come
Home at five in the morning
And go straight to the bathroom
And turn on the water to do
Whatever you needed to do
Before you came to bed to me
All cleaned up to lie beside me
Don't think I didn't notice that
When you slipped into bed
You slept on the other side
Far away from me and all the
While I held my composure
With my head under the pillow
Whispering motherfucker
Knowing that I would have
Done the same thing too

Motherfucker

Point Taken

How silly of me
To be so in love with you
How irresponsible of me
To completely deconstruct
Just because of you

Rebirth

I walked in the church full of naysayer's
Christian paraplegics and holier-than-thou's
Quickly erasing my being to fit into
The midst of 400 Sunday fashion models
From a distance I feel his eyes on me
Beckoning me to drawn in rebirth like
The night before last and the one before that
And almost every night
We lay next to each other; aligned
As his wife lay's across our chests
Burdened by time lost, distant memories
And a vague sense of mold
When she speaks in tongues
His eyes are heavy with trust
Hungry for what's behind closed doors
My heart feels light somehow
The gods have swallowed this sin and
Regurgitated my filth on a boulevard
In my escorts womb
I stepped in my recovery mourning
Bewildered, tired and withdrawn
I heard it again
Then again, once again
Just like the night before last
And the one before that and almost
Every night since this began
He wants me to drown in rebirth
As we lay aligned, tongue-tied
With the weight of his wife's breasts

Heavy on me weighing me down
Wondering when he'll be home
I stepped in the tepid water
One hand on my head inches from my heart
One hand on my back feeling every emotion
I drowned in his rebirth wondering how
I could ever love another man
Drowning in a pool of water

Catch and Release

You think you got me
Like some crab in a barrel
A fish stuck in a glass jar
Think you will feed me
When you want to
Polluting my water with
Flakes and poison
Go ahead
Dump, pour, fill
I know how to survive
With the sharks
I know how to swim with the fishes

Color Struck

The color of your garment
Black like tar in the night
Pitch black eyes
Grayish almost black lids
Shuffling around like the
Dead and praying someone will
See you in the distance
You walk like the
Movement of a flashlight
You are moonstruck and just
Wandering in the night and
Wonder why I don't see you
Won't let me see you exposed
Won't allow me to see
What loving you is like
Your interest in me lies
In you dreaming that I'll be the color white
Transparent so you can blend in with me
Hoping you and I will by accident
Merge into each other and become
Grey and stuck in love with one another
Grey, dull, bored, settled and done
And ready for you and I to
Disappear out of sight
Hoping our grey feet become stuck
In this fickle soil of the earth
Hoping I will surrender and become
The shade you have made me
Realizing that every time

You touch and merge with me
My color never returns
Realizing your color overpowers
Every part of me
Realizing that is all you
Ever wanted us to be
Every bit of me merged with you
Every color in me must become
The color of you
And you wonder why
I'm unsure if you are
Really ready to love a color like me

Whip

Keep showing up
And raping these
Thoughts in my
Dreams and I'll
Show you what
Submission is
Really all about

Vow of Silence

It's quiet in this house
Too quiet if you ask me
Thought I was supposed
To be meditating but I can't
Get you out of my head
Wish you were here
Sharing this silence with me
Wish you'd get out of my head
And stop screaming how much
You love me in whispers
But I must admit I love how your
LOVE is silently deafening

...And Then

You...at the greyhound station
Not knowing where to go
Lips tight with a lot of
Luggage/my luggage
Photographs falling from your
Pockets staring at you like
Yes, you were with me and
Yes, you are what
Everyone thinks you are
Photographs spread-eagle
Somehow falling in order
Of our history, a mystery
How we lasted that long
Its ok, I'm just going to
Stand here and watch you
Run off with my luggage
Get on that greyhound bus
And go nowhere but somewhere
Far away from me...maybe L.A.
Who knows, you did always like
The feeling of the sun
Photographs just lying on the
Floor all scattered about for
These passer-by's to walk on
Similar to how you did me
Thinking...

"Where's this man going with all that luggage?"
"Hey Mr., you dropped some things."

You look down or the faces
From the photographs look up
No, you looked down
And maybe had you not looked
At me in those photographs
All naked and exposed the way
You had many times before
I wouldn't be standing here waiting
Hoping I could tap
You on your shoulder
And say let's go home, you win
Never knew your feet moved so
Quickly at the site of me
I must remind you of what happens
When mistakes become reality
Not sure how much longer I can
Stand here watching
You hold on and grip that
Luggage and try to leave
Yea, maybe had I just let you
Win that last argument
We'd be at home right now
Your feet laying in my lap eating bad
Chinese food with plastic forks
Because we never learned
How to use chopsticks
Sitting settled admitting to each other
That neither one of us is apparently
Smarter than a fifth grader
I wait and wait patiently for some

Explanation why my feet are
Planted here in this greyhound station
Watching you leave me with these
Photographs on the floor and
My luggage in your hands
Finally you tell me it's over
Like I'm some character in a
Play you just wrote
Some antagonist who lost
The battle trying to win the war
You say it's over so poetically
Quietly like a whisper that
I never heard a word
You wait for this awkward
Moment to be over so
I won't notice you're leaving
With my luggage gripped tightly
Our photographs on the floor
And I want to tell you
That you dropped
Our photographs on the
Floor...dropping me

Remember when we stood outside
New Years Eve cold and frozen
Hot chocolate $1.50 I think...
You and I, hmph that was something huh?

That night was going
To be our memory
This sinking battle ship we

Called love played us like a fool
And we succumbed to that thought
And loved it like it was
But clearly never meant to be
And just like that it's over
No sequel, no next time...over
You've got my luggage so
No need in wondering where
Your bus is going but hey man
You dropped some photographs
Maybe you just want to
Leave this memory behind
The bad taste in your mouth...me

Haiku

Did not know I could
Be stuck inside myself and
Feel completely lost

Two

The
Cri De Couer

PROPANE

I could break this shit open
And fill it with pink dust
And aint it funny how pink lust
Make niggas fly with broken wings
Broken wings make em fly
Into skyscrapers with no parachutes
Playing strip poker with life lines
Spreading lies in hieroglyphics like coke lines
These niggas get so high off the rush
They pass spirits in the field of greed
Camouflaged with the scent of musk
Can dot dot dot com and download
Dirges on an I-pod touch
These niggas pump lead
And ejaculate like puss
So funny how these girls
Fall for a happy meal
And a pass on the bus
Yeah a pat on the butt
Made her spread eagle
Spread out on her mama's
Plastic covered couch
Screaming and praying for the baby
Waiting for nigga to bust
She said he sexed her so good
She used his words like a back shot
She overlooks the ledge
Where suicide acts as a backdrop
So disgusted she stands still

Believing that if her soul
Went to heaven God would reject it
And hell would be her last stop
Cuz it's a long road back home
For these lost southern girls
Who have wandered away
On dirty back roads
A long way home for these lost girls
Who dream of kneepads
With protective guards
Cuz honestly church girls don't
Always wanna give the dog a bone
Fiends of dope girls don't like
Stripping on the pole
Don't wanna know what it's like
To tell mama she's bringing
Another baby home
Doesn't quite wanna think about
Raising a daughter of a daughter
Having a daughter on her own
And these are hard pills to swallow
When raised by a whore
Hard pills to swallow when
Raised on molded bread and tap water
So sick of eating with the rats and
Roaches so she gets high and hallucinates
On thoughts of abortion
Her vision has become so distorted
Drowning in a bloodbath
Wading in the water
She contemplates not

Wanting to be a mom
Of these bastard children
Forces herself to believe
Getting rid of this sin
Is sort of like a master cleansing
So she rocks her abdomen from left to right
Not because of the life inside
Not because of the life she'll let die
Not because this sin will
Be dead by next weekend
But all because she realizes her
Womb is a graveyard full of semen
A womb full of un-scattered cremated ashes
A gravesite that's full of bastards
Cuz they don't built her up
Smacked her back down to a low level
And wrote her off on their taxes
Left her looking for hope
Broken and tilted on her axis
Reality bites when you
Gamble profit for assets
These girls all looking for
Love from men who
Just needed the practice
Experimental love and life
Must be so attractive
Reaching for plastic and jelly in a basket
Forming seeds of bad habits
Dumping dreams in a casket
Lining coffins with the plastic
No need in spreading of the ashes

Surrounded her sin 6 feet
In the ground full of maggots
Dumped dirt on top of this
Supposed love like dad did
Growing the green up
The vine like a cactus
Read epithets from
The church pamphlet
Broke down cuz she
Really couldn't stand it
To be wanted, used and
Then left abandoned
Left her feeling like
Respect is just not demanded
There's just no understanding
Why trade your right to be left-handed?
Especially when you'll just cover up
The truth with a bandage

Labor Pains

This is my life
And I just don't
Want to die tonight

The Morning Breath

Its 8:46 in the morning
46 minutes past the time
I was supposed to be up
I realize you and I have
Falling in to a groove
So comfortable that I stop
Asking where you were last night
I stop thinking why you
Are never here with me
I don't even consider
If there's someone else
You're keeping company with
I just hope you brought home
Some eggs so I can make u breakfast

Jazz Blues

Sitting in the bath tub
Washing the dirt off of me
The filthy residue from you
Listening to Betty Carter ask me
Whatever Happened To Love?
And all I can think about is
Whatever happened to YOU?

Feathers

I am lonely again
And again, my pillow
Is taking your place
Replacing the space
Where your body should be
Why are you so damn unavailable?

Pulse

I'm waiting in bed
For you to come home
Hoping this dream person
Will appear because honestly
The idea of u loving me
Keeps me from jumping off this cliff

Dust

The wind blows you
Clear away from me
You are useless and
That's why you can't
Be with me

Room Service

I lay my head on a purple pillow case
Ralph Lauren I think
It covers up this hotels bed bug pillow
And I guess this is my mornings
Slice of humble pie
So I get up and find a fork
No doubt left from
Previous tenants who had
No choice like me
Yeah, extended stay aint so bad
It's better than being homeless right?
Nah, just one in the same
So I sit, I stare, I eat my pie
Until I'm good and full
I lay myself back down
Think, think, thinking
How I got here?
How the hell am I gonna get out?
Aint no use in crying cuz
I can't mess up my pillows
And the maid only comes once a week
She doesn't speak English and
She doesn't understand that
That spray in a can
Aint gonna clean everything
Aint gonna clean up this mess I made
That smelly shit in a can
Can't undo the fact that
I'm almost thirty living in

An extended stay hotel
Because it was better than being homeless
Nah, just one in the same
Can't quite get myself to sleep
That dog next door keeps barking
Can't quite hear myself think so
I contemplate getting up and
Going next door to knock
Before I realize I can't
Really do that because she's
Not, you know my neighbor
She's just another person in
The same predicament as me
So why shit on her day by
Telling her I can't sleep
Why shake it up for someone else?
Why disturb this groove we've fallen into?
Why not just let her sleeping dog lie?
I turn off the TV, adjust my air-conditioner
Making sure I get my $29 a night fix
Making sure I kill these bed bugs
Making sure my humble pie
Is cool for the touch
Making sure I'm all set and ready to
Lay my burdens down if
For only one night
In my deluxe extended stay
Home away from home

Wind-Up Toy

As we sat we paid
We played the game
I swayed him to every beat
Of the song and we danced
And after the conga drum beat
We slept and there was no wife
No other man, no separations
No divide, no lingering on color lines
We saw us, me from the north
He, birthed from scotch and a dream
He became beats and I ad-libbed
On a pulse he left on my sheets
Overdosing as he made the song
Cry out of me

Thrust

I'm in this predicament often
Every night I feel the urge
Sometimes with the
Early morning dew
And with just a
Few strokes of the pen
This thrill is gone again

Distant Lover

Just know that while
You were gone
Somebody
Had to keep
Me company

Fly Away

If we were to ever meet again
I would still want to marry you
And have kids with you
Knowing that you never
Loved me

Broken Promises

You told me
You would call me
When you got home
It's been three years
Where are you at?

Urgency

When all is said and done
Water under the bridge
We still lied about our
State of complacency
We couldn't even admit it to ourselves
Nothing has changed
And it's time to move on
We only have ourselves to blame
It went on too long and
It's too late to get it together
Way past the mend it stage
No hard feelings
No hurt emotions
Just lets be something
We never were...friends
Let's say goodbye to
What we had and welcome
The future of separation
And yeah, I know it will be hard
And at times too much to bear
But what do we have to lose
We've been fighting this
Losing battle for too long
And I don't know about you but
I'm tired of you and I being
Something birthed out of convenience
And I'll admit it, at times
I started arguments maybe to
Prove a point or for

No reason at all
It'll be hard and
I'm sure there will be
Lonely nights in the
Near future when I wish that
We never had this conversation
And I'll have to wrap
Myself in the warmth of
Good times and old memories
It's lonely being alone
And love is lovely when
You're in love but we're not
So let's just be done and over already

Room 1011

We lay in bed in a tiny hotel room
You asleep, me wide awake with desire
I scan the room where I find
$300 sneakers on the carpet
That you just had to have
$150 pair of jeans that you
Love so much
And the one thing in this room
That I need so bad is unattainable
Love should never hurt this bad

Haiku

Hey be my sex fiend
Be my midnight closet freak
Does it feel good yet?

Haiku

Head above water
Lonely and molested nights
Dead but still breathing

The Fix

Your body convulses
Under the weight of me
Your grip slowly weakens the
Pressure cooker inside of me
Easily our bodies mesh
Together to become we
Our grasps crash and collide
Forgetting how to breathe
Quickly your fingers spread and
Grip the sheets to slow the screams
How easily your legs twitch and
Succumb to my regime
Tongues lick the spots
Around and in between
This back and forth teasing
Only revs up the machine
I inhale and exhale the smell of you
Something like a fiend
We finish and allow our
Bodies to lean into each other
All intertwined as we
Lay under the covers
We are something undefined
No titles, not really lovers
We never hesitate to call
When one needs the other that's why I
Allow you to roam free around this continent
Seek, find, play and discover

Sight Seeing

I stand still
One mirror in front of me
And one in the back
I see all the faces and I wonder
Which one is confident?
Which one is carefree?
Which one is loveable?
Which one is a risk taker?
A free soul that flies
Any way the wind blows
Which one is sexy?
Which one is me?
Which one made me fall in love with you?
Which one did you adore?
Who is the one you left?
Which one is the one that made you unhappy?
I move, I sway side to side
I try to find some truth behind
The reason we're over
I notice all the faces in the mirror
Answer all the questions for me
                    It's just me, it was always me
Wasn't it dummy?

Maybe Tomorrow

I don't wanna write today
Don't wanna dig up bullshit
And put it to paper
Don't wanna waste
Time on these feelings
Don't wanna admit to everyone
That I fell in love and as such
I held myself hostage to someone
Who left years ago
Someone who left me broken and
Searching for pieces of the old me
Pieces of me I didn't know were
Alive and available for loving someone
Who had no care for me
Don't wanna admit to my mother
That she really is right that the
Light behind my eyes has faded
And I have no idea how to get it back
Don't wanna tell my older sister
I know I have a soft place
In her heart and admit that
I know her sisterly advice is
More love than judgment
Can't tell the middle one
I'm jealous and envious
And out of everyone it's her
Attention I want the most
Can't look my nephew in the eyes
And pretend not to notice

I might let him down
I might become the product of
The men who raised me
Don't wanna admit to my
Closest friends that half of what
I told them was what I
Wanted them to believe
That I have no idea who I ever was
And who I think I want to be
So to me it's easier being
Someone more acceptable
Someone more unlike me
I don't wanna pick up the phone
And call that woman in Brooklyn
The woman who I love more
Than the language in my mouth
And tell her I'm not as polished
As she thinks I am
Can't admit I had no choice
Who I love and don't really know
Where I lie in my faith and
I worry about what I'll do when
I can no longer hear her tell me
She's proud of me
So no, I don't wanna write today
I don't wanna dig up bullshit
And put it to paper
Not today

Three

The Smoke Screen

Target Practice

I bet you never thought you would
Drown yourself in this ocean
Never thought you would wrap your body
Like clover around men who lay
On top of your dreams
For an hour of escape from reality
Didn't think men would find
The rainbow in your bosom
The sway of your back leading
Them down to the river
They rock your hips so gently
Just to find your color
You're kissed with silver tongues
Caressed with metal hands
That holds you down
They leave remnants of their stay
Like lava on your gown so other men
Can smell the odor as they pay by the hour
And whisper something in your ear
No doubt a voice similar to your father
I bet you never thought you had the
Opportunity to survive in this ocean
Never thought men would leave
Your bed with you still in it
Never thought their bodies would leave
Imprints on your pillows the shade of black
Didn't think you would be so fragile and
Left fractured searching for that image
In the mirror that once reminded you

You were pretty
There's no guessing how you will
Survive in this here big city with men
Who line up adolescent bodies
Like coke cans and aim for an attack
I bet you never thought the sound
Of the pendulum in the clock would
Crack and drag you second by second
To your death wishing his grunts
Would speed up and finally
Explode like a gunshot
Never thought men would roam around
Your continent digging up
Your past in dirty soil
Planting new seeds of growth
Ideas that laying down next to
Another body giving away freely
The water in the well would
Be your definition of a woman and it's sad
Watching another girl from around the way
On a block just around the corner
Fall victim to the belief that there is
No choice left but to drown herself
In this ocean and hope she will float to the top
And pray for redemption that
Some god will take her away from
This world full of grown men
Who just wanted her for an
Hour's worth of target practice

Post

In the past winter you passed by me
With your belongings in your hand and
Told me you were leaving
Told me you found
Another place to be
Another soul to dwell in
Another meal and a
Place to rest your feet
The following summer you
Returned home to me
Waiting patiently
Waiting for a soul to dwell in
A hot meal and a place to rest your feet
And in the timeframe of one minute
While weeping at the knees
Even you admitted a flashing sign
Doesn't always mean there's a vacancy

Sound Bite

If I can regurgitate
This filth in some
Willing prostitute's womb
What would be the reason
I would hold on to you?

Go Please Stay

It's not that I'm not feeling you
You're cute and I think I like you
So maybe we can work
Something out
But then again, I'm unsure
We are different and opposites
Do attract so let's just do this
But I don't know
Let's just wait
Let me think about it
I think I'm unsure
You and I are two boats
Drifting apart
Together, side by side
Behind each other
Underneath, on top
Aligned, separated and
What I'm really trying to say is
It's not going to work
I think, maybe…… ughh

Haiku

It's only when I'm
In a mood he strips me down
And gets in my groove

The Honeymoon is Over

He used to bring all the
Angels to the community
And sprinkle em down like dust
A drip in the IV called lust
Used to make the fiends break out in hives
Shit, piss, the stench of musk
Street pin kingpin like Dudas
Could sell the rumble in
The garden like Rucker
Making these niggas walk like
Egyptians clutching co-pilots
Falling down all chalked up
Leaving you breathless
Behind the velvet rope
Made you believe purchasing some
Shit in a vial would give you hope, nope
But who these niggas gonna believe?
A street prophet that walks like a god
Or some scribbled words in the book
And that's a lot to consider staring at the
Spoon waiting for that release to cook
Looking death in the eye of the shotgun
Blue heaven banging like a drum
Blow by blow until the pain is numb
Amped out hoping Aunt Hazel will return
Cuz Aunt Mary always promises
A yellow sunshine will bring fun
Laid out on their backs blowing

Blue kisses at the sun
No worries mama's got a dream gun
Letting Mary Jane's sister
Creep up in em during sleep
Aint nothing wrong with walking
Corpses in the streets
Victims swaying back and
Forth to the beat
These escapes feed like a
Buffet bar with all the fixings
Can conjure up the spirits
To mix a special elixir
This party is an invite only
Not some after hour's mixer
Only for the advanced players
Betting closed for beginners
Best believe this potency will
Sure nuff' leave your body disfigured
Aint no words gonna save you
When they coming from the minister
Nothing these needles don't already
Communicate with the visitors
Everyone plays by the same rules
Of the game in the streets
The suits, the pimps
The players and the whores
Everyone's accepted and
Entitled to play in the score
It's just a matter of rolling up
Your sleeves to enlist in the war

She Say Oooh...

I wanted to write some hot shit
That produced a spark in her spine
So divine like the pinnacle
She would say it's clinical
How my words sound so biblical
A timeless journey that make my legacy
Overshadow my swagger and seem cynical
Even though I'm ughh
I can still make her say oooh
And for that she's ridiculed
Sometimes ostracized seeming pitiful
She says oooh
Every time I make her feel the burn
I make her high I'm her tequila worm
That feeds off of air every time she uses me
As a life support to fix her yearn
A respirator with functions to make her
Emotions do epileptic turns
Everything's so magnetic
I'm so ughh but she's gotta have it
She's got a man calm and collected
But she's caught up and dreamy over me
Erratic, wild and drastic
I like to puff
And even though she huffs
She likes it rough
That's why she's so tough
She says oooh
Every time I fill her cup

Never more than she can take
But more than enough
She's at the edge but
I won't let her jump
The energy she gives me
Is such an adrenaline rush
She makes me blush
Just the thought keeps me in awe I hush
She said oooh and I could feel her pain
I asked her name
But her voice had no range
She stood and I noticed the change
She walked up on me
Whispered in my ear oooh
And that ended the game

Confusion

She said I had
Sex appeal
A sex symbol
But I didn't
Appeal to her
Sexually

These Interruptions

Woke up, dressed, forgot to brush my teeth
Sink drains....hurry
Sweep, dust, and get everything out the corner
Drive, smile, greet...be
Live the lie to make this money
If this is my life, my rules
Why can't I make the choices?
Eat well, eat alone, eat, eat, drink, and guzzle
Pray one more day, one less pound
Walk, burn, feel the sun
He's on his way
This last but for a short time
Drive, ride, rush hour accidents arise
Someone's not making it home tonight
Home; watch, rest, read, pray
Think, sit still, and watch the clock register time
Iron, press, wash, clean, breathe, think
Someone loves me in this world
Alone all over again
Comb, change, do it again
Adjust all pillows on the floor
This comfort, too comfortable
Toss, turn, get up, water; heartburn
Reflection in the mirror warns me
I can't do this much longer
Relax, look again
Bed, sleep
Morning time....do it again

Spoiled Brat

I'm good aint I?
Good at being your spoiled brat
Super cat doing my knuckle buffing
My Mr. Bojangles shuffling
Said that you loved me for being
Your rock and I guess that's why
I waited so patiently
Do you love me baby?
Did you ever love me?
You ever plan on loving me?
Do you care? I mean
Do you even like me?
Do you even understand?

Weekend Routine

On Friday I went to sleep
Clutching my pillow
Believing it was the
Warmth of some body
Saturday I met you
Sunday we were in a
Relationship having relations
Monday no calls, no texts
Tuesday back to clutching my pillow

Crutches

When I asked him if he
Even knew how old I was
He said maybe in your early thirties
And if he would have said
He really had no idea
That would've explained
Late birthday cards that I never
Received or why he used
To beat on mama or why I
Only heard from him here and there
It would've explained it all
But he didn't. It didn't.
When I asked him
When he would start claiming
Me as his he said
I don't know, too many question
And if he would've said
Soon son, very soon
It would've explained
Why he lived in the bottle
And nourished his veins with cocaine
But he didn't. It didn't.
When I asked him if
He ever loved me or ever
Thought about me
He told me he would have to
Speak with me on another occasion
Because he had to clean his dirty laundry

Encore

I know that staying here
Taking just one more
Phone call from you
Exhausting all the possibilities
Opening up this door just once again
Letting you wear
Out your welcome
Sweeping dirt in front
Of my door again
Will lead to no solution.
I know if I allow
One more call at night
From just one more
Insecure adolescent parasite
Telling me with whom, what
And where you've been
I know I'll fall victim
And that will just allow you to
Break my heart again

Home Remedy

I'm gonna grow dreadlocks
And play on my guitar...yeah
That'll help me get over you

Death of Winter

I hear these birds chirp
And I know that spring
Is on the rise it's no disguise
You're working it out in the gym
Waiting for these flocks
Of geese to arrive
These dirty fossils break you
Off and wear you out
With their hives
Even mocking birds drop like
Pigeon shit from the sky
These parrots lay eggs
And spread germs like flies
They hibernated all winter
Woke up dressed
And marched in line
It's hilarious watching these
Grapes crawl up the vine
Pull you back down suck you off
Laying with the beast on their spine
You push they pull back
Easy enough for you
To spread their thighs
You must love the larva
These winged creatures
Leave in the pie
These vultures love to wreck
Homes and tell lies
It's so simple to lay traps

And spread pesticides
Leaving crumbs waiting
For these pests to die
You desperados love to
Attract desperate followers
Vultures that drop dead like cicadas
Sniffing the sweet nectar
Off of the flower
Hiding out in the bower
Licking poison from the lips so sour
All packed in fall for spring showers
These cowards pray on a
Weather change for power
Love to exchange fun
An exchange rate for the hour
No use trying to pull the
Moth out of the fire
It's the flicker of the flame
These dead logs admire
A ritual in the spring for the
Birds to jump in the pyre
They swear they've evolved past
Swinging on the spire
But fall dead when these
Primates get tangled up and
Caught in the wire

Unfinished Business

You think because
You dance in poetry
You can write my life
And think you know me
You think you know
My rhythm and can
Feel the vibrations
When I walk and see
The future in my steps
You think you can measure
My pulse and know how
Fast it beats but wont
Realize it was you two
Who left me drowning
In the sea

Prototype

They say he
Looks like me
And acts like me
I guess that's
Their way of creating
A younger, better
Version of me

Conditionally

We can wake up together
Go to sleep breathing
Next to each other
Can stay on the phone
Late nights with each other
Cry a river and swim deep together
Can create dreams and
Live out loud together
Dance, sing and just
Be with each other
We can share the same space together
Bank accounts excluded
No exchanging one for the other
Make memories the first of
Many with each other
Argue, fuss and fight with each other
Make up and do it
All again with each other
There is no denying that
You and I belong together
Living happily and in
Strong like of one another
But loving you, that wasn't
Part of the equation
And I can't quite recall us
Ever having that conversation
Never haggled, never had negotiations
Didn't know loving me
Could create complications

These emotions make for such
An uncomfortable situation
How could trust
In a four letter word
Lead to this here confrontation
And I won't deny that
I have grown some fixation
Having you around made me
Work through some frustrations
Should have known this
Honeymoon was just probation
And honestly, had I known
That being in love with you
Was a just cause of sublimation
I would have made it clear
From the start that I would only
Be with you on a conditional basis
So for arguments sake
I'll just admit that I love you
And hope that being vulnerable
Means that you and I
Never have to discuss
The conditions of our separation

Intervention

A few spirits came to visit me
Old ancestors from afar
They told me I was dying
I was in love with finding love
And it was killing me
Said they never saw
Something like this before
We sat and discussed my behaviors
They gave me ultimatums
Told me I needed their help
Set a plan of action for me
Told me withdrawal was necessary
I asked if they have ever been in love
And they told me they had
Died for the same cause
And it was all so foolish
I told them if they gave me more time
I could find a love just for them
They sat in silence

Haiku

Loving you is one
Hell of a drug that's why I
Always overdose

Rocket Ships

You and I became the first in flight
Left on a midnight train from
Georgia late one night
The pair of us were joined
At the hip so tight
Never thought our spaceships
Would love to fight
Thought we were matched just right
And I remember the way
You looked in the light
A burning rage in your eyes
Shined so bright
Saw forbidden fruit from the apple tree
And took a bite
Saw the life we were dreaming of
Fly away on a kite
Beyond belief how these skies began to lie
We were what everyone
Else thought they liked
Never yielded or stopped
When we saw the signs
Didn't think to safeguard us for the climb
And after this up and down
Galaxy ride you still wonder why
Our rocket ships crashed and died

Four

Confrontations

The Long Way Home

They knelt at the pulpit to get
Cleansed from the Deacon his cup
Runneth over with young boy's semen
Said he was touching them to
Cast out all their demons
Dreamt he had a prophecy one night
Felt he had cause to
Save these heathens
Such a righteous cause
For a beast and a cretin
A sham, a crook, a fraud, a legion
Broke bread with Rev'rn as
He watched them eat em
Sure enough them black birds
Gonna come back for the reaping
Knew they were the sacrificial lambs
With every fiber of their being
How easily they became the
Communion Sunday for the season
No yellow brick road
Paving their path to Jesus
No guide, no map
No light, no beacon
No right, no wrong
No rhyme nor reason
No flowers for this funeral
From the Garden of Eden
So cleverly disguised
This ritual of desire

Wanted something new
Something untouched
Something fresh with no priors
Waited until they were of
Legal age no longer minors
Summoned to the captains
Quarter's where he retires
Told them to be still and keep quiet
And no one would be the wiser
Felt pain in a quiet place
Splitting legs open like wires
No usher, no elder
No altar boy or choir
No one would believe these
Little black children over a liar
He was after all
Their religious advisor
Another co-conspirator
Misreading passages from the bible
They couldn't see a way out
Not given a master plan
No water, no fire
No path of footprints in the sand
It's mimicry behind this cloth
Posing as a man
What a wonderful mask to
Wear for all his faithful endearing fans
The crimson and cream must've
Mistakenly carried the
Dirt across the sand
Settled his debt out of court to

Wash the blood off his hands
Perjury must be the biblical
Measure of this man cuz
All these peapods in the pews
Invested in his brand
There's truth in a lie
A notion they just can't understand
How quickly he painted himself
Out to be the victim
As he walked out the church
Holding the hand of the misses
A rogue with a no lye relaxer
Better fits the description
He preached about them boys
Who was just out to get him
All their ill will to get
Closer to his pension
Heard them New Birth followers
Fell on the floor at the mention
Their road to kingdom come
No longer paved with good intentions
And no one thought to
Make some different decisions
No one thought to question
Any of his henchmen for fear
The prelate would hang them
Out for the lynching
But there's no way you can blind us
We see right through them
Expensive designers even though
Your Christian 10 percenter's

Paid for your blinders them rose
Colored glasses only serve as reminders
This is what happens every time
We believe the church is behind us
But in god we trust that the truth
Gonna come spilling from your gut
A sanguine mess dripping your
Homo/hetero tendencies in the cut
A disgrace that the church haphazardly
Put their faith in a mutt
A misappropriation of the funds
To support his habits of lust
But that Savannah Band
Said it the best
Everyone's the same
All the saints and the sluts

Evolution

Back in the days a look from
A parent was enough for a
Child to realize boundaries
Were crossed and a quick
Behavior switch was imminent
These days a look to a child
Is an invitation for the
Click of a gun
BOOM

Acid Trip

I sit shotgun hostile with a shotgun
Breathe in earth and air and
Watch it collapse in my lungs
I'm hot son hot as Hades
Burnt under a black sun
Humdrum I assimilate in my mind
Sit back and pop gum
Standing on a soapbox all supped up
Aint ready to preach from the pulpit
Got balls balling in the court
Don't know how to survive in the bull pit
Cockeyed cocking the gun
Sniffing ether in the cockpit

Ughh

So I'll never get married
And have 2.3 kids
Cuz the lifestyle I live
They say aint shit but sin
No, I'll never knock up a chick
No arbitrary notches on my belt
But these words come swift
And my delivery is felt
Fuck em if they call me names
And say I'm wrong
Cuz I'm strong and piped up
In an atomic bomb
Humbled and weighed down
In a gravity tomb
Thorough and long awaited
Like the PS2 and
I'm not your king conqueror
Brooklyn boxing ya
Down to the cock blocking ya
Tits in the tube socks in ya
Harlem show stopping
Minstrelsy globetrotting
With a good diddy bop
Harlem shaking pop locking ya
And my body was not made to be
Fucked and torn, raped and sore
And I'm not your downtown poor
Shit talking hard core
Hourly paid whore

In your bodega corner store
Not your corner block bitch
Street smart hood rich
Living in the ghetto Lexus driving
Late bill payment arriving
Success thriving
Dollar bill lying
Screw face eyeing
Nickel bag buying
Minimum wage job applying
Not your Sunday sinner
Guess who's coming to dinner
Not your Pride winner
Ebonics talking finna
Copper complexioned
Close to henna
Not your ATL balla
Ur Kingston shot caller
Not your queer as folk poster boy
Your jailhouse pussy boy
Not your G unit hustler toy
Project booster or buster
And I'm not your Ughh

Big Bad Wolf

These black Jesus' like to preach
And talk in circles pull up their
Britches snort and laugh like Urkel
They sit back and amaze themselves
All these black Christopher Columbus's
Trying to conquer some shit that already existed
Re-telling prophecies a
French seer already predicted
Funny how they send black threats
To a black president in a White House
With mixed constituents a mixed
Bag of nuts all these skirts in suits
Running around like mutts in blood money
They trust these upper echelons dirt's crust
Sins of greed and lust and it's a must
These Know Nothings do something
Pretending to be blind to the touch
A Wall Street adrenaline rush
Pundits so repugnant hiding behind
A kangaroo court secret
Operation Paperclip just for sport
They speak in circles
They laugh from their bowels
They huff and puff and
Wipe their crap with a towel
Shoot to kill when the
Small hand hits the hour and
Wash blood from their
Desensitized hands in the shower

A disgusting tradition passed down
Through the hands holding power
Superpowers with sweaty palms
In secrecy on MK Ultra
No wonder they prey on victims
Hunched over like vultures
How quickly they thought the
Epidemic would crumble our structure
These scare tactics only further insult us
Cause we see right through
All your missteps and blunders
We was raised to be some
Panthers when we were youngsters
Always taught to save
The beast from the hunter
Leave his ass to die in
The wilderness from hunger
Let em hear the clap of
That roaring ass thunder
Send out a smoke signal for them
Other wolves and tell em it's supper
They eat till' your body is drained from all color
Dispose all the evidence in the project dumpster
Leaving your smelly ass
Rotting away in the gutter
Never thought them hands would
Shake hands with the other
But that's what happens when
Dirty deals are done undercover

Off With Their Heads

I can write a line in rhyme
Read it in Braille and
Perform it like a mime and
That's a warning that this beast
Will feast whenever he dines
That's sort of like the seventh sign
Cuz even these dyslectics will connect
All these dots to form a parallel line
These locusts will have you
All believing lies like the
Truth aint the tie that binds and
I'm guessing they're blind
They keep killing themselves
On my poison ivy vines
I am the prelude to the sequel
For anyone trying to disrupt my sermon
Its communion so you will be baptized
Leaving these non-believers
Wailing out like bees at the hive
These neophytes fall on bended knee
Praising Baal's and deity's
Bribing with tithes
I am the bird-clap in the hood
The death sentence waiting
On the corner like a drive-by
I need not mention I buried
All these henchmen
Men in skirts all suited up to get lynched in
I don't need to say I'm number one

I'm second to none and that's
One leg up on the competition
I am the wire fence separating
The masses by the border
No one's allowed to amass
Their wealth on my corner
So I drop bombs over Baghdad
Leaving em dead in the water
Bringing the guillotine down
For these cowards who falter
I accept all these disenfranchised souls
To be beheaded at the altar
And keep all you headless bastards
Locked up and rotting away in the coffer

Animal Testing

These New York men are lab rats
Specimens who want men with
Flat abs and six packs
Don't want shit fast-tracked
But want you prepared
With condoms in the backpack
Claiming they want a lab animal
On the right path
Watch and set the attack with cheese
And see them run for the mouse trap

Elsewhere

Use somebody else
Go ahead and bleed in someone else
Sleep, lie and live with someone else
Dream on, dream big with someone else
So glad you ran off with someone else
Crash and burn with someone else
I suspect you will ruin this someone else
Happy you can pretend to love someone else
Mature and grow with someone else
Hope you can admit you needed someone else
A shark in the water will always
Feed on someone else
How quick you will turn into someone else
Cuz the real you loves to
Pretend to be someone else
Misuse and abuse this someone else
I bet you think this song is about you
Believe it or not this requiem is for someone else
Hope you bought a bulletproof vest
For this new someone else
Can't wait to see you
Massacre someone else
How easy it was to
Flaunt your new someone else
You two will do a great job
Lying to yourselves
Catch a grenade pull the pin
And detonate yourselves

Guerilla Theatre

Smuggling E-pills, tits and junk in the trunk
With two dumps getting that heroin pumped
Girls got knocked when the semen dropped
Niggas got popped
When the block got hot
Crack spots
Guerillas preying shotgun in the drop
Feds beating down the average man
The streets most loyal fan
Fiending for contraband
Seizing niggas like the Taliban
Niggas killing each other
Using blood as spray paint
Yelling revolution
Like it's a fucking mission statement
Chillin on the corner hair napped
Hooded and dressed out in the Gap
Half-baked with a roc in the hip
Hypnotic Harlem shake
Young ones in school learning ABC's
With their 123's on Mac-11, 9's
And if you're blind my language will be
Signed, sealed and opened
Imported, exported, extorted
By anthrax specialists
Sending warning letters
Rockin' a bullet proof sweater
And it aint no secret
We be more powerful than

Osama Bin Laden with LSD lace-up shoes
Minstrelsies bleeding on rags
Sporting Gucci bags
Selling vials out of pants that sag
Running out of time
In new Air Jordan's
With kick me signs
Freedom cries
Too hot in the back of the bus
So I'm just gonna chill here for a minute
Nah B we don't suffer from insanity
We enjoy every minute of it
Every minute I represent dollar signs
With faces of triple 6 minds
And we've been americanly/confederately
Capitalizing on Benjamin's
Since they had small faces
Marker marked in the corner
To spot the hidden watermark traces
And I know hot it be
We eat so much bullshit
On a regular day basis
Conforming to ideas
That everything tastes like chicken
But everything that glitters is gold
Like the steel shackles when we were sold
But that story's untold
730 believing the game is old
Cuz street love is cold
With society in a choke hold

Missing Ingredients

You better take notes
And doctor some transcripts
Learn how to do what we do
This craft is food for thought
Knowledge you won't find in food
This thing we real poets do
Aint for the faint of heart
Basically this shit aint for you
You sheep in cheap kente cloth
Act like y'all got something to prove
Imposters studying poetry books
Scrambling and looking for clues
Learning to recite
Their bought incite on cue
Nothing edifying in these diatribes
Nothing worthy of putting into view
Broke and can't afford to pay their dues
Created a blueprint how to win
But aint really thought it through
Can't handle the temp in the kitchen
Burnt from the bitches brew
A bunch of sous-chef's
In the kitchen fucking with the stew
Something old something new
Something borrowed and blue
They won't admit it but
These niggas bit off
More than they can chew

Done started a war but
Didn't really follow through
Faux poets having minstrels
Bleeding crap on pages
Blood all soaking thru
Vision completely askew
So tried and true
Something missing
Lost in the sauce
Lost some links
Missing a few screws
Can't see the vision
Even with a bird's eye view
Won't survive this cipher
You pseudo's just come unglued

Out The Box

Some people live in
Small houses on a
Small plot of land with
Small windows and
Invite me over to sit
On their oversized sofa
To share their
Small ideas with me
And wonder why
I never come over to visit

Learned Behavior

All of these birds didn't fly south
These crows feel like
Death in words all
Stuffed in my mouth
Set up shop in front of my house
They tell me of barrios
Where school girls play hopscotch
TIC TAC TOE sucking on lollipops
They practice rhythm
With hula hoops eyeing birds
In cuckoo clocks
Sticking out pinky's with
Cocaine on it till time stops
They give away their virginity
For quarter water's and dime bags
A chemical reaction like stardust
Making these boys stare
Wanna double dutch
And spin the bottle like Star Search
It's a blind thirst
Sort of like a blessing in a curse
Cuz these kids can't be kids
When playing in dirt
They idolize and dress baby dolls
Until that turns into birth
Mama taught anatomy
But never net worth
Pops was MIA or
Upstate at worst

But what can you say to
These Hello Kitty girls
Who like to learn in spurts
Wasn't a night she wasn't
Tucked in dreaming of desserts
Smiles from boys, LOL's and flirts
Flirts from boys who could
Facebook and face time
But couldn't read or rhyme
Could recite poetry
While getting head on a pipeline
Puff, pass, flying so high
Waiting for these oxygen masks
To fall out of the sky
Cuz these Johnny apple seeds
Yield to grown man
Johnny apple needs
Rocking these love and hate rings
Posted up like Radio Raheem
These kids learn life in the streets
Not raised to be Huxtable teens
And their dreams all
Crushed and chalk outlined
Trying to be a microphone fiend
These beasts suck the
Life out of these leeches
A bunch of misguided
Poor righteous teachers
They bleed these streets
For Jordan sneakers
These kids don't grow up

Dreaming of stocks
They dream of a big bang
Crip walking and
Banging on the block
And this generation of youth
Has no fear in their hearts
They were raised by
Sitting bulls and learned that
Clapping, surviving and
Breeding was an art
Leaving indelible stains
Of semen like graffiti marks
They grab hold take your money
And put a gun to your wife
The grab hold fill the chamber
And put a gun to their life

Five

Battle Scars

The Thrill Is Gone

I find that as I get older I have become
Less agreeable and unwilling to take just whatever
Comes my way and attach the name of love to it
I no longer sleep on any side of the bed
I prefer the middle so I don't remind myself
Just what love did and roll over and
Sleep next to nothing
I no longer get rosy cheeked when complimented
For fear I might find that after all
I too can be vulnerable
No longer wondering what will
Happen with "us" five years ahead
Forgetting to just live for this moment
I have realized though that I
Do have something to offer
Something more tangible than a
Fuck in some public place exposing
Myself to the humility with you
Can't hide the fact that I have questioned
And do question and will continue to question
If I have ever been in love
Like real love and not the idea of
What I thought it should be
I am easy like Sunday morning and I have
Found in my growing and maturation process
That I have fallen out of love with love
And honestly, I don't know when
I'll ever know just what it all meant
And what the big damn deal was

When the Smoke Clears

See, I'm just gonna sit here and
Let these drugs take effect
No need telling tales of
Loves lost and old flames
Gonna sit still and marinate
Sour in these juices I've made
Had this heart of mine broken so many times
I can't be sure the blood runs freely

Basic Instincts

I'm human and I guess that's
Why I loved you so much
I foolishly let go of myself
Because falling in love with you
Was more than enough

Haiku

I'm glad you left, now
I have time to focus on
Getting rid of you

Gravity

Mountains move all around
Easily fading into the scene
A diamond in the gravel
Unaware of what it means
A voice can get lost in the
Distance of violent screams
The plain view shifts out of focus
And gets blurred in the dream
Everything in this world has fallen in between
Flat lining to the rhythm
Of the pulse on the monitor screen
Admittedly there's more than the
Mass that forces it to be held down
The way the garment is worn and
The luster missing from the crown
It's the echo everyone hears
In the middle of the crowd
The apparent cry for help
Becomes disturbingly loud
The err in the steps is like a blueprint
For the mistakes that have been allowed
Thoughts make it seem like there's more than
Enough to join the spirits in the clouds
There's an unfulfilled purpose brewing from within
The light at the end of the tunnel
Is reflective in one's skin
But all that's heard are the voices from
The flock asking where you've been

Give the Drummer Some

The music stopped playing around us
We became lost in our own song
And that became dangerous
How both tunes became synonymous
Caught up in our rapture so oblivious
Standing in those waters with you was treacherous
You and I in the same sentence anymore
Simply preposterous
Ashamed I allowed you to introduce
Me as anonymous
Shame on you foolish on me
To become your accomplice
Swallowing these lies like a virus
Pretending like the truth would never align us
Remaining faithful and having faith
Two thoughts that would never find us
And aint it crazy how the perception
We made up started to blind us
Believing this shit like a truth serum would bind us
Loving you became an infection that made me
Wanna play that track again because
It skipped over our beat
But let's just face it
This tune is past its season
We were a one hit wonder
Not worth repeating

Oui C'est Tout

We met and it was
Love at first site I bet
We talked and courted
We were in love I guess
You were there I was here
That was such a mess
Two people who really
Didn't know what to expect
You're back I'm happy
Now here comes the stress
What will really happen
When we put this to rest
We walk and talk
I laid my head on your chest
That moment I swore
Was divinely blessed
You drop a bomb amid
A commitment to invest
I am yours and you
Are mine nevertheless
You're just a plane ride away
Or so you expressed
We tried and tried
And gave it our best
I can finally admit
I was somewhat obsessed
Anything you wanted
How quickly I acquiesced
The more I advanced

The more you regressed
I was your hidden secret
Your reliable largesse
Thought moving you in
My space was viable progress
I know now that you were
A cause and after effect
To love unconditionally
And receive no respect
They say time heals wounds
But you never forget
Time has allowed me to
Look back, think and reflect
I'm finally piecing back
Together all the disconnects
Our unfinished business
Was the last part
The last piece of the
Broken puzzle to address
I salute you for succeeding
In what is considered as
My life's biggest regret

Ready

You try as best as you can
To make me believe that
Here is not where you
Really want to be
You swear someone else has
Stolen you away from me and is
Waiting for you to hurry up
With this supposed break-up
To return home to them
But honestly, if this dream
Person really existed, you
Wouldn't be spending so
Much time convincing me
You want to leave me
So tell me, when exactly
Do you plan to start loving me?

Haiku

The way you left me
Left someone to leave you
Now how does it feel?

LOVE Huh?

I didn't even get a goodbye
Not even a note on the table telling me
I was the worst boyfriend you've ever had
No phone call with you screaming at me
Cursing and crying only to hang up on me
We didn't sit down mediation style
To see if we were going to be
Able to salvage the remnants of
An already broken relationship
We didn't seek counsel from god
You and I never even attempted to pray about it
Didn't get an opportunity to
Go to couples therapy to see
Somebody with no insight and no interest
In our relationship could
Guide us in the right direction
I didn't get the time to tell you
How I felt or express what would
Happen to me if you left
No pictures left to remind me what love can do
Not even a
Take care, keep in touch, this will be good for us,
Someday we will be friends hallmark card
Didn't have anyone there to rescue me
And I couldn't even call anybody
Couldn't bring myself to tell anyone
That you left and probably weren't coming back
Nothing, I got nothing but an
Empty apartment and time

6 years worth for me to sit
And wait for this death to be over
And then the numbness set in
No tears, no cri de coeur...nothing
Falling out of love was like
Slipping inside myself slow like death
Veiled and fading into black
Those once jittery butterflies
Emerged from their cocoon and
Eroded in my stomach like maggots
And no one talked to me about
What to do when it's done and
Where to begin after it's ended
And now after the hurricane has
Come and gone, I'm not even sure
If me investing my time in this
Notion called LOVE was worth it at all

Night Vision

Some higher power already
Predicted our future
He was looking at us tearing
Each other apart through
A telescope using a magnifying
Glass watching us slip down the
Hourglass timing our demise

Fine Print

I have unlimited minutes
On my phone so
You have unlimited time
To find you a new place
With unlimited possibilities
Where you can have over
Unlimited visitors
And those unlimited visitors
Can do whatever they want
With a limitless being
So start calling because I've
Just reached my limits

Next Episode

I slept alone last night
Just like the night
Before last and
There is no use
Wasting ink on you
Because inflation
Is on the rise so
Turn to the next page
Immediately

Spray Cans

Heard them bricks was peeling
Caught the tail-end
Behind an abandoned building
Started to tear the roof off the ceiling
Envisioned a bloodbath of
Fathers, sons and innocent civilians
Hired them boys overseas
Separated the masses by millions
It's an eerie feeling
Commercialized to make this shit appealing
Can't help that getting high
Evokes some feelings
Brought it to the forefront that
Those founding fathers were stealing
And no one thought to ask
How we were feeling?
Can still smell the pine sol scent
Of piss in a hollow hallway
In the projects building
Passed by an old man with a
Stained collar from a lassoed neck
Wanted to inject some knowledge
In me hoping I would reflect
Told me he found his place here
And that earned him some respect
Didn't think to stop, pause, ask or interject
Said he found out I thought I was
Some kind of brain child
Some sort of intellect

Questioned what I would do
When them good ole boys
Wouldn't allow me to intercept
Thought the past presents
A future of no regrets
Knew I was better than a thief
A junky, baby daddy or rape suspect
Heard them gunshots sound off
Like a sound effect
Wouldn't duck, never moved
No need to catch my breath
Approached by a fiend with a
Gleaming smile rocking to her death
Promised me dreams in a staircase
Stopping traffic like a bottleneck
Said 5 to 10 dollars
Would get her wrecked
Gave her food and left her stranded
Told her to get some rest
Left her nodding like a dreamer
Saw these niggas out front
Wandering like lemures
Dead men walking
Peddling weed for beamers
A separation of red and blue
Hung from back pockets like streamers
Two worlds apart, a divider between us
Kept thinking that this
Grass should be greener
Wish the world outside
My window looked cleaner

These red and blue colors
Argue black on the green
No wonder the blood of innocence
Drips thick and swims up stream
Bloodshed at a block party
Taped off as a homicide scene
They drop the blanket over the body
In front of his mom as she screams
A promise that nothing in
This life is ever as it seems
Can't stand to watch the
Blood run down the block
Thinning out into the concrete seams
No fair being young black and gifted
If you can't survive this scene
This pavement won't embalm these cadavers
What they call savage behavior
We call routine
Our yellow brick road graffiti'd over
Matching souls spray canned bluish green
A road full of crack vials and
Boys using needles like vaccines
Foreseeable how they get trapped
And caught up in this machine

The Pace of the Young

It was there in
The subway tunnel of the
D train heading back home
A muffled voice told
Me that the love that
I had been fighting for
Was the wrong love for me
The love I had been
Hoping for should be
Taken away from me
Hard to hear the truth
As the conductor speaks
But it was there on
Our way back home to
The Bronx that my
4 year old nephew snapped
Me back to reality

Haiku

If you want to be
In love with me build a bridge.
Learn how to cross it

Sniffing and smelling myself

...At the tire shop
Smelling the burn of tires
Thinking I'm so tired of you
Running through my mind
Tired of you running
Over me leaving marks
Leaving tracks that remind me
I smell like burnt rubber
And everyone since you
Can smell it on me too

Man Down

Yeah nigga you an
Idiot for that shit
Letting that nigga creep up
Inside you for so long
Letting that muscle decay
Like a carcass
Left you stranded in your
Own desert you created
Rolling like a tumbleweed
Broke you down till you were
Hot, dry and dead...

Life Support

I ask myself what I will do
At night when these
Stray bullets with
Social security numbers
Etched in steel come
Flying past my window on
Tremont Ave, Boogie down Bronx
On a cold winter night waiting
For the hour of death to pass me by

Where is your life man?

If someone out there finds it
Deliver it back to me
Buy a stamp, steal an envelope
Press your lips to it so
I know you found it and
Wanted to keep it
But knew it wasn't yours
Fold it up, crease it evenly
Stuff it in and make sure it fits
Seal it; make sure to lick the back
Press down hard
Drop it in the postage paid box

Where is your life man?

If someone is on time for their night shift
It will be sorted, needs to be sorted

Dropped in another box
And passed through hands
Passing through more hands
In route back to the hands that let it go

Where is your life man?

Where is this life you keep talking about?
Where is this
Rising
Walking
Talking
Breathing
Needing
Thirsting
Crying
Elated
Loving
Wanting
Prideful
Freeing life?

When you find it
Hold onto it
Breath it in and
Inhaleinhaleinhale
Inhaleinhale
Inhale
Inhale it...live it and BE it

Six

Closing Arguments

Lost In Translation

Will they talk about me
When I'm old and in a
Nursing home strapped to a bed
With dirty linens looking at
My color TV wondering
What happened to all the real people
Or are they dying just like me?
Will they wheel me around when
I smell of fetid urine and
I'm lost in my own memory and forget
That I was once somebody
Some wild child arrogant in youth
Fun, alive, fresh and free?
Will they remember that I was
Once LIVING in this place
A place not suitable for men or
Will they just remember how much
I bitched about not wanting
To leave this place?
Will they even remember me?
Would they have brought me
To the lake to soak my feet
In murky waters or bathed me
Until the black washed off me
And I became a shade
More suitable for acceptance?
Would they have listened?
Will they no longer whisper
About the boy who thought he

Was too good to be some suit and tie
All dressed up for a cubicle
Staring at the clock
Waiting for 5 to come remembering
His mother once told him to
Live and love, laugh and dream?
Would I have learned anything
In the time I was here
Useful enough for me to survive
In another life, in another place
More peaceful than here?
Did I ever cross paths with someone
In life who was thankful at my smile
That reminded them everything
In time would be ok?
Will I leave behind a legacy at all?
Or go down as another somebody
Just lost in translation?

Seasons Change

Someday I'll be 80 years old
And I'll pull up in my driveway
I'll park the car, open the door
And you'll pop into my head
I'll reminisce about our past
And remind myself
Why it never worked
I'll laugh to myself
You know the same laugh
I promised myself in my youth

"I'll look back and laugh
About this when I'm older"

And I will do just that
Laugh at the thought of us
Laugh at the hint of us
Smile because I know I
Made the right decision
Leaving you was bittersweet
But getting over you...
Just as lovely as I thought it was
Overdosing on my drug of choice
Overdosing on you
No better than coming off
My high like methadone

Secret Society

Its times like this
Moments in the midst
We gather and I feel the love
I hear the laughter, I see the smiling faces
Men of confidence who decided out would
Always be better than in
We are the generation
Of leaders and molders
Who set the standard
There's love here and
Family and everything
In times like this
Moments in the midst
Everything is erased and
I know it's ok to just be me

Hush

Word might get out that I
Have fallen in love with men
And the masses will show up at
My door with crucifixes
Holy water and garlic cloves
Ready to recite bible verses
That begs me to live in secrecy

Sun Showers

I remember weekend mornings
Dr. Buzzard's Original Savannah Band
Playing in the background as you
Cooked scrambled eggs, grits and bacon
Cheese wiz in my eggs cuz I was
Your baby and I liked it that way

"Hey kids, food's done wash your hands"

Never knew why the dog liked me
So much around breakfast time
Oh well, I gave her bacon anyway
I remember your perfume, that lingering smell
The way you dressed with class so poised
Silk, satin and sequence and only
Applying makeup to enhance what you
Already had and I remember loving you
More than my CAT in the HAT stuffed animal
I remember your backbone, strength, resilience
Back then I remember you in church
Praising and worshipping instilling in me
That faith was possible
Out of all the hero's to choose from
He-man, Care Bears and such
You were my one and only
Always been, always will be
I remember being held at night
While you caressed my eyebrows

How quickly I fell asleep
I remember you singing to me
Comforting me, assuring me that
I'd have all the joys in the world
I remembered the way you danced with me
And I knew somehow we would always
Dance together and now I'm all grown up
And were still dancing together
You have always been, will always be
Forever in this world and the next
My one and only woman
If for nothing else
I owe you a kiss for everyday
For every school play attended
For every band aid on every scrape
For every time you became two parents
For teaching me right from wrong
For always and forever
Being my sun shower

Love always
Doo Doo head
Kiss #10,585

Haiku

I AM WOMAN and
She was, strong proud and sassy
And I knew her well

Security Blanket

He holds me and I sweat
The smell of sex funky
Endures the pain and
Years of heartache
He leaves urine on the toilet seat
And I feel at home
He takes a shower and I join him
Cleansing away the
So many disappointments
That promised they would never be
He kisses me and I melt
Laughs and I cry
On the humble I need him
And I'll never let this dream die
When I'm in his presence
Accompanied by basketball
Bawdy jokes and beer
And his words drip with
Disdain and male superiority
I feel a comfort that
Only true intimacy can bring
I wash the dishes and
Clean his dirty clothes
I feel at peace
I feel secure and
I am finally in love
With just me

Blues Baby

I've got these two lovely ladies
I call them sister one
And sister two
They drive me up the wall
And I wear them out
With my blues
They'll never know how
Much they mean to a
Wanderer like me
It's the walk in their steps
This effortless air
That they breathe
It's the heir about them
The way they
Laugh to the beat
They are the hills up yonder
And the water underneath
Those ladies of mine
Sister T and Sister C
Boy they sure can drive
Me up a wall but that's
How I like them cuz
They're looking after me

Redux (29-35)

I realize that I have changed
Still changing
I've gotten a little older and
Things don't fit the way they used to
The evolution has begun
The deconstruction still in progress
The reconstruction about to start
I've checked in
Put an X on some realities
No longer in that age bracket anymore
Did some soul searching and told myself
      "Hell, there aint nothing wrong with ya"
Cleaned out my closet
      "Don't know why I ever liked this...
      Can't believe I'm still trying to wear this"
Looked back
Laughed at old photos and bad hairdo's
Lost my faith and found it again
Something has been revived in me
I'm growing, becoming the man I've always
Wanted to be, always thought I would be
Silently thanking the three birds
Perched on my window that raised me
Women themselves who have
Already braved their resolutions
Yes, everything is gonna be alright
X marks the spot and I'm ok with that

On The Writers Block

I wanna write a poem
Where my words drip blood
Like a lyrical syringe
Where metaphors eat similes
On virgin paper
That masturbates to ballpoint pens
A poem where peoples mind intent
Is so blown away that they
Call my flow manifest destiny
Describing how my word schemes
Flow through blood streams
Full of catch phrases and punch lines
A poem where my words synchronize
Everyone's tongue to silence
Where I blow dust
To make third eyes
Have cataracts and
20/20 vision so abstract
I wanna write a poem
Where sonnets bungee jump
And hyperboles Kris Kross jump
Pull up to my bumper baby bump bump
Where actions speak
Louder than words
Where meters hopscotch
And checkmate prose
I want the thoughts of idioms to
Rape the alphabet and molest lyrics
Where oxymorons lie naked

Next to haiku's and
Have wet dreams of
Pronouns fucking adjectives
I want sestinas to fall
In love with pronunciation
And ideas question mark punctuation
I wanna write a poem
Where my synonyms are
A continuation of my antonyms
And jealousy lurks behind
Bushes of acronyms
Where nouns are hip-hop
Beats are singular
And sound is verbally abusive
Where syllables peak octaves that
Only a deaf man can hear
The type of poem where
You get hunger pains
From knowledge seeds
I wanna write some
Hot shit you see
The last of a dying breed
The definitive poem
The Johnny apple seed
Cuz its gotta be on my terms
My time, my way
I wanna write a poem where
Swagger is multidimensional
Composed and *it was written*
Where thoughts have heartbeats and skip beats
Failing needing respiratory resuscitation

And words cut veins like ginzu knives
And noose's rope tie life lines
Where literary terms
Can't breathe, no breath, no air
Where sparks produce flames and
Poet's pseudonyms have no names
I wanna write a poem where symbols
Imitate Braille and patronize Yale
And dance in circles around
Spoken work paraplegics
Piece by piece, line by line
I need, I crave I feel like
I really wanna be a poet today

Here It Is

I could write my life story but
Who would read it?
I would script ten thousand lies
And you'd have to believe it
Make a billboard out of deceit
Just to see it
Junked your veins with tries
Food for thought
Now you gotta feed it
I could cry a liver
Break down and sing you a river
Weightless weight quicksand
Stand and deliver
I could be bold, brash
And act real bitter
But if I gave in
You would break and call me a quitter
I could curse, kill and die in jail
That might make you glad
Be a product of environment
Scapegoat cuz I had no dad
To re-read my life resume
Might make me sad
But this is it, here it is
This is all I have

In The After Hours

The lord came to speak to me
In soft audible tones
Like frequencies
Told me I was never meant
To be passed over but
Passed down in descendancy
He needed me, wanted me to
Fulfill my purpose urgently
Told me the masses had
Already heard of me
They were delivered messages from
The folk in past lives in ancestry
It's a gift you see, it took my hand
On your shoulder is what he told me
Told me to become a shock value
And shake it up like epilepsy
Pay no mind to any controversy
He stood in front of me and told me
If I took time and had patience
I would be the last of a dying breed
And that's a lot you see
A simple kid from uptown
Given a warning that I better
Get down and deliver this prophecy
Gave me insight into
What the prophets see
I started not to believe
Until he grabbed hold of me
Stood me straight up looked me in

The face and told me
You're not going to find
What you're looking for in
Any book written about poetry
Shit don't come in no DVD
Won't experience the extent of
What I can do listening to some gospel cd
And yeah it was profane but sometimes
That's what happens in deliveries
A shiver in my spine when
He speaks to me
Son things aren't always going
To be given to you when
You want them sometimes you're
Gonna have to work with me
I come to you at night and
Can't predict your dreams
So do me a favor sit down
And start writing for me
I replied I can't my king
I aint got no food for thought
I've been writing in poverty
Feeling a block in my mind feverishly
I'm in despair and need
Your comfort desperately
I couldn't help but notice his doubt in me
I was like a mockery
Given a destiny with a roadmap but
Couldn't fulfill my duties
Can't break away from the dependency
Can't muster up the courage

To be all I can be
His warning finally came
Down on me like the guillotine
Get your hands off and
Invest in the power of me
I wouldn't have given you a gift
If I thought you couldn't succeed
Exhale, relax and learn how to breathe
Everything inside you
Will need to be freed
Put your pain in the pen and
Watch them pages bleed
No use in having a voice if
You don't know how to speak
No use in having these abilities
If you don't know how to teach
Use this vision as an insight
Inside of what the impoverished need
Feed these wandering souls poetically
Never think, don't stop
Do this constantly and when
You're tired and need a break
Push harder for me because
What you have son is
Something so unique
Pay no mind when you get
Visits from the enemies
Trust that all these haters will
Act up and act out in enmity
Never stray or get off your path
Put your foot in the sand and

Walk right next to me
Trust in faith and the gift
That you were given by me
You must always believe
In the powers that be
I've provided the blueprint
A guide and all the
Ingredients for the recipe
So do me a favor son
Sit down and just start writing for me

Haiku

Joy comes early in
The morning, learned that in the
Process of mourning

Acknowledgements

      This project has been a long time coming and I have no doubt in my mind that it is because of God that I am alive, breathing and able to share my story with everyone.

      There are a lot of people that I need to thank for helping me along the way and constantly encouraging me to finish this book. I certainly wouldn't have been able to do anything without my family to support me. To my mom Beverly Cole, there aren't enough words in the world to describe how much I love, appreciate and adore you. We promised each other that we would always dance and we still are dancing and we always will, I love you. To my sister Tiffany, thanks for showing me that the real me was better than what everyone thought I should be I love you. To my sister Christine, thanks for encouraging me to always do my best and to never accept less than that I love you. To my sisters Tanya and Shanegia, who knew time would make everything come together? I love you dearly. To my Aunt Ruth, you are such a driving force and motivation in my life, I don't know what I would do if I didn't have you in my corner I love you. To my Aunt Denise, it's always refreshing to know I have a home away from home and love that I can be free with you I love you. To my uncles Herman and Gary, I wouldn't trade you for anything, love you guys. To my nephew William, I'm glad that I can watch you grow into a young man I love you. To my nephew Justin, you are the reason why I am still here. You mean more to me than the words in my mouth. You are becoming a young man and I see myself in you more and more and I'm privileged that I have the opportunity to be a part of your life, I love you.

I really do believe that I have some of the greatest friends in the world. I don't know how I would have survived without you special people. You all are slowly showing me that I can be ME and I love you for that. Kyvaughn Brown, you are truly the funniest person that I know. You keep me young and I am so glad that I met you. You have truly added to my life, I love you. Brandon Coates, you are the liveliest and most free spirit that I have ever met. You are so talented and I love you for being a great friend to me. Courtney Williams, you and I are inseparable. It doesn't matter if you and I end up on another side of the world, our bond is unbreakable, and I love you. Donta Morrison, you are so talented and I am honored to have a friend like you. In a short time you are a friend that I look forward to always being in my life, love you brother. Jamal Powell, I swear you and I must have been separated at birth. You have always made sure that I knew I was special and I love you for seeing something in me that I didn't see in myself. Jason Wallace thanks for being a great friend and always having my back, I love you. June Glover, I don't believe that I will ever meet someone like you again and I wouldn't trade you for the world.

You have shown me that it's okay to have a voice and speak up and I'll never forget that, I love you. Keith Lockwood, you are simply the best. It doesn't matter what I do, I know if there is one person I can always come to for support it's you and I love you dearly. Lynn Houston, thank you. You have shown me that there are people that care no matter what and I'll never forget that. Makeda James, you are the best. I know that if there is one person in this world who will never pass judgment on me, it's you, I love you dearly.

To Weylann Tarver, Toure Lewis, Lorian Hill and my grandfather Herman Cole, I miss you so much. I know that I have angels in heaven watching over me making sure that I will always be okay. I miss you and love you always.

There would be no way that I would have been able to right this book if it weren't for YOU. Thank you for making it all possible. I thank you for breaking me down and showing me the truth. I hold no more resentment and I wish you the best. This is the last piece of the puzzle between us, the last war I will ever enlist myself in. And finally this is it, this is our LAST EXIT.

Made in the USA
Monee, IL
16 May 2022

96528364R00085